The Fourth of July

Written by Sonica Ellis

Illustrated by Nejla Shojaie

Copyright © 2022
All Rights Reserved

ISBN 978-1-7372647-8-1

DEDICATION

This book is dedicated to Liam and Finn.
May you always be each other's best friend.

Croakers Creek was home to a lot of critters. In this lush and beautiful community there were turtles, swans, and dragonflies.
This is a story about Duck and Frog.

Duck and Frog had been best friends since they were small.
They did everything together.
You never found one without the other.

It was the day before the Fourth of July picnic and Duck and Frog were playing in Duck's room.
"Duck," Frog said, "I want to do something nice for our neighbor Mr. Turtellini. I don't think it's right for him to be all alone on the holiday."
Frog continued, "Do you have any ideas of what we could do?"

"I'm not sure," said Duck.
"Perhaps we could save him a plate from tomorrow's picnic," Frog croaked.

The two were so engrossed in their planning that they didn't see Duck's mom standing in the doorway.
"Good idea," said Duck.
"But what if we just invited him to the picnic instead?"
"Would your mom and dad be okay with that?" Frog asked.

Just then Duck's mom entered the room.
"I think that's a brilliant idea!
We have more food than we could possibly eat," she said.
"I just love how you both look out for others."
Duck's mom hugged them close. "I hope you never change."

So, off they went to Mr. Turtellini's house to invite him to the picnic, but Duck and Frog soon discovered that Mr. Turtellini wasn't home. Just as they were about to leave, they saw Herman Snail.

"Hello, Mr. Herman," said Frog. "Do you know where Mr. Turtellini is?" "We don't want him to be alone for the holiday so we want to invite him to the picnic tomorrow." Duck added.

"I saw him walking down the road not too long ago," replied Mr. Herman. "Thank you!" Frog said.

Just then Duck had an idea.

"Mr. Herman, would you and Mrs. Herman like to come to our Fourth of July picnic tomorrow as well?" asked Duck.

"Why, we would love to!" Mr. Herman replied.

"Great!" shouted Duck and Frog. "We will see you both at noon." Then off they went down the road in search of Mr. Turtellini.

Next, they saw Sheron Heron.
"Hello, Mrs. Sheron. Have you seen Mr. Turtellini?" asked Frog.

"We are trying to find him so that we can invite him to our Fourth of July picnic tomorrow," said Duck.

"I saw him not too long ago," said Mrs. Sheron pointing, "right up that hill."

"Duck," whispered Frog, "perhaps you could invite Mrs. Sheron to the picnic too. She and her son could use some company. What do you think?"

"Frog, I think you're right," said Duck. "Mrs. Sheron, would you and your son like to come to the picnic as well?"

"How very kind of you!" said Mrs. Sheron. "Baron and I will be there!"
"Great!" replied Duck and Frog. "We will see you at noon."

And so it went. Duck and Frog invited everyone they saw to the picnic until they found Mr. Turtellini at last, sitting on a stump overlooking the pond.

"Hello," said Mr. Turtellini. "I heard you two were looking for me and I would love to come to your Fourth of July picnic. It is kind of you to invite me. Thank you."

"Great," said Duck and Frog, "We'll see you at noon."
and with that they hurried home
to share the news with their parents.

The next morning, Duck and Frog woke early to help their parents peel potatoes, mince onions, squeeze lemons, roast nuts, and chop carrots. Together, they made sandwiches for the picnic.

By the time they had finished and changed their clothes, all the critters had started to gather.

They each brought a little something for Duck and Frog. Everyone ate and told jokes and stories.

And in the evening as they watched the fireworks, they all thanked Duck and Frog for being so kind.

Made in the USA
Las Vegas, NV
09 June 2022